FANFARES AND PROCESSIONALS

EIGHT PIECES
FOR ORGAN

BY

MODERN COMPOSERS

NOVELLO & CO LTD

CONTENTS

1 INTRADA

BRIAN BROCKLESS

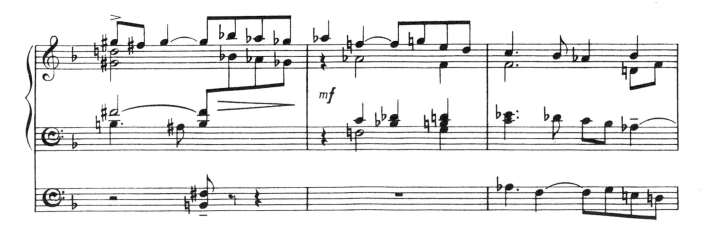

rall.   poco a poco accel.

* A change of manual may be made here, if desired; returning to G♮ at †

poco rall.

a tempo

add Reeds
più f

allarg.

meno mosso   più allarg.

ff

fff

For St. Michael and All Angels

2 FANFARE

Solo to be played on Tuba, Tromba or Trumpet
on any convenient manual.

GUY H. ELDRIDGE

MANUAL

PEDAL

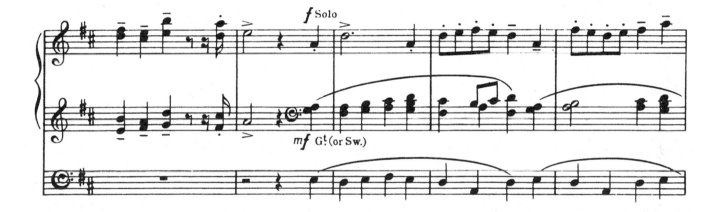

3 FANFARE

I Solo reed
II Chorus work (to balance)
without 16′ manual stop

TONY HEWITT-JONES

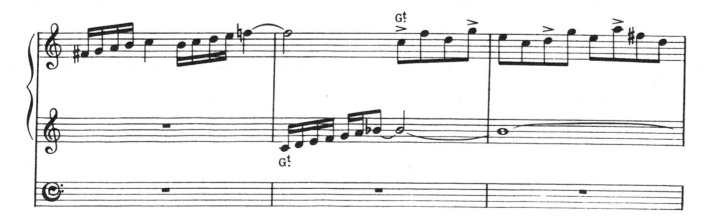

accel. poco a poco

Allegro molto ♩ = 152-160

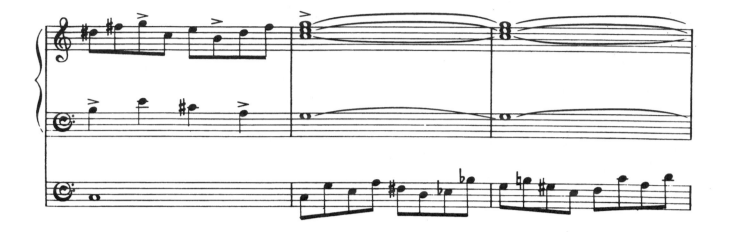

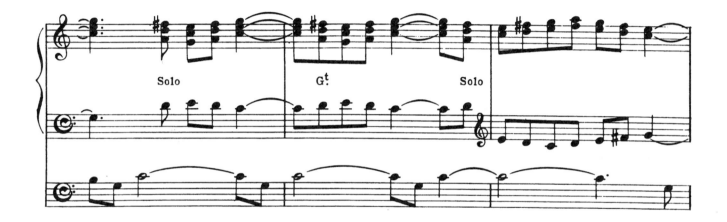

4 FANFARE

C. S. LANG
Opus 85

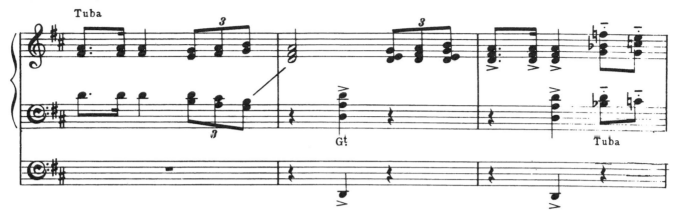

5 TWO SHORT FANFARES

ERIC H. THIMAN

I

Pomposo ♩ = c. 110

MANUAL

PEDAL

II

Allegro ♩ = c. 80

6 SOLEMN PROCESSION

LLOYD WEBBER

rall.

poco accel.

add Sw. reeds

cresc.

accel. sempre

Tuba

cresc.

Tuba

allarg.

accel.

(box open)

f Gt

cresc.

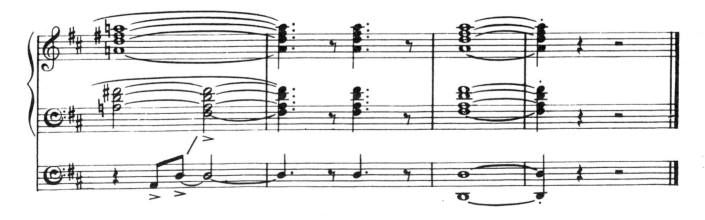

For Colin and Rachel

7 FANFARE

I Solo reed
II Chorus work (to balance solo)

ARTHUR WILLS

Tempo I

FESTAL VOLUNTARIES

These six albums, intended for particular Church Seasons, each contain five pieces based on appropriate hymn tunes. Despite the use of the word 'Festal', provision has been made for the season of Lent and Passiontide. All the pieces were written specially for this series and the composers have assumed a wide interpretation of the chorale prelude form, the various styles including Prelude, Interlude, Postlude, Sortie, Meditation, Rhapsody and Pastorale.

ADVENT

JACKSON, Francis
WACHET AUF

LANG, C S
WINCHESTER NEW

ROWLEY, Alec
CONDITOR ALME

LLOYD WEBBER, W S
HELMSLEY

STATHAM, Heathcote
VENI EMMANUEL

CHRISTMAS & EPIPHANY

COOK, John
DIVINUM MYSTERIUM

LANGSTROTH, Ivan
WINCHESTER OLD

THIMAN, Eric H
ADESTE FIDELES

PEETERS, Flor
STUTTGART

HARRIS, William H
DIX

LENT, PASSIONTIDE & PALM SUNDAY

THIMAN, Eric H
HORSLEY

GILBERT, Norman
ROCKINGHAM

SLATER, Gordon
HERZLIEBSTER JESU

RATCLIFFE, Desmond
PASSION CHORALE

WILLAN, Healey
SAINT THEODULPH

EASTER

HARRIS, William H
EASTER HYMN

SLATER, Gordon
ST FULBERT

LANG, C S
VICTORY

RATCLIFFE, Desmond
WÜRTEMBURG

PEETERS, Flor
LASST UNS ERFREUEN

ASCENSION, WHITSUNTIDE & TRINITY

WILLAN, Healey
ASCENSION

COOK, John
VENI CREATOR

ROWLEY, Alec
HAWKHURST

GILBERT, Norman
LAUS DEO

GRIFFITHS, Vernon
NICAEA

HARVEST

GRIFFITHS, Vernon
ST GEORGE

STATHAM, Heathcote
MONKLAND

LLOYD WEBBER, W S
HOLYROOD

LANGSTROTH, Ivan
WIR PFLÜGEN

JACKSON, Francis
NUN DANKET